Bezzler

Half-witted and always hungry, a Bezzler's favourite food is Frickles, but it will eat anything it can stuff into its grubby little mouth.

fig 1.

fig 2.

fig 3.

fuzzle

Ju-Ju-Juicy Bong Tree

The Ju-Ju-Bong's juicy leaves are a cool refreshing snack for thirsty animals.

fig. 1.

6.

Enigmatic Desmond

yum yum

Quinch

fig 1.

fig 2.

Crest

fig 3.

Hapicriss Moss

The Borks' main food, this bright yellow plant forms an edible carpet that covers most of Charleebob's surface.

These playful bird-like creatures spend their days guzzling Ju-Ju-Bong juice and their nights getting up to go to the toilet.

For Charles Darwin, for explaining *how we all became* – JE

For ducks, llamas, centipedes, giant clams, pterodactyls and moles,
along with all the other funny-looking creatures
that helped me illustrate this book – ED

Text copyright © Jonathan Emmett 2018
Illustrations copyright © Elys Dolan 2018

First published in Great Britain and in the USA in 2018 by
Otter-Barry Books, Little Orchard, Burley Gate, Hereford, HR1 3QS

www.otterbarrybooks.com

A catalogue record for this book is available from the British Library.

ISBN 978-1-91095-919-0

Illustrated with watercolour

Printed in China

1 3 5 7 9 8 6 4 2

How the BORKs BECAME

Words by **Jonathan Emmett**
Pictures by **Elys Dolan**

Otter-Barry BOOKS

On a faraway planet, quite like our own Earth,
a bunch of Bork mothers has just given birth

to a great brood of Borklings, in all shapes and sizes.
Some look like their parents – but some are surprises.

The thing about Borks is, no two are a match.
They're **all** a bit different, just look at this batch.

Sniff!

These odd little differences help the Borks thrive.
Without them, it's doubtful they'd still be alive.

You see, Borks haven't **always** looked as they do.
Their fur was once short and its colour was blue,
and those long, skinny necks that make them so tall
were once very squat and not skinny at all.

This might start you wondering, wondering **HOW?**
How did the Borks become what they are now?
What caused all these changes? What brought them about?
Well, we'll have to go back a few years to find out....

On a faraway planet, quite like our own Earth,
a bunch of Bork mothers had just given birth
to a great brood of Borklings, in all shapes and sizes.
Some looked like their parents – but some were surprises.

While most of the Borklings had fur that was short,
there were also a few of a shaggier sort.
These shaggy-furred Borklings, they looked kind of funny
and got rather hot when the weather was sunny.

But later that year, when the weather turned chilly,
the shaggy-furred Borks did not feel quite so silly.

While the shorter-furred Borks couldn't cope with the storm,
their shaggy-furred cousins kept perfectly warm.

And when the storm stopped and a new day arrived,
only the shaggy-furred Borks had survived!

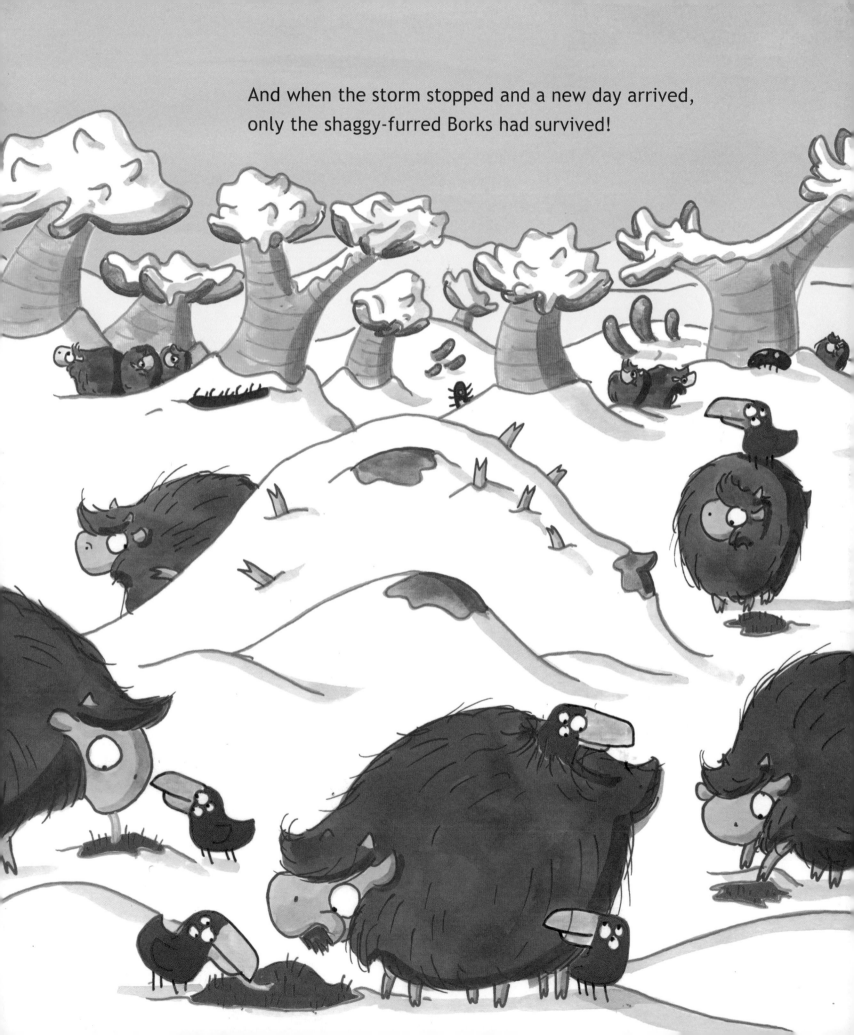

So the next time a big Borkling birthing occurred,
all of the babies were born shaggy-furred.
While most of these offspring were bright shades of blue,
some were bright yellow, but only a few.

These bright yellow Borklings looked rather bizarre
and weren't very easy to spot from afar,
as their fur blended in with the bright yellow moss
which covered the plain that the Borks roamed across.

They were roaming this plain on a hot sunny day
when a **Ravenous Snarfle** came flying their way.

Now there's nothing a Snarfle likes more for its lunch than a beakful of Borks . . .

so it snatched up a bunch!
It gobbled up every last Bork it could find,
every last one – but it left some behind.

The big beastly bird would have gobbled the lot,
but the bright yellow Borks had been too hard to spot.

And so, when the next batch of babies came through,
all of the offspring were yellow, not blue.

But, while most of these Borklings had necks that were squat,
there were also a few who had necks that were not!
These skinny-necked Borklings looked rather absurd,
with their heads towering over the rest of the herd.

But later that year, when the weather grew dry,
these tall Borks were glad to have heads up so high.
For without any rain the moss shrivelled up dead,
and moss was the food on which every Bork fed.

So with nothing to eat, many Borks died off too,
almost all of the herd, except for a few.

For the skinny-necked Borks things were not quite so dire,
because, thanks to those necks, they could reach a bit higher
and feed on the branches of Ju-Ju-Bong trees,
which held lots of water within their thick leaves.

So we're back where we started, but now you know **HOW**.
You know how the Borks became what they are now.

And if anyone asks how this mystery is solved,
you can tell them the answer – they simply **EVOLVED!**

It's truly remarkable, wondrous and strange,
how through **EVOLUTION** a creature can change.

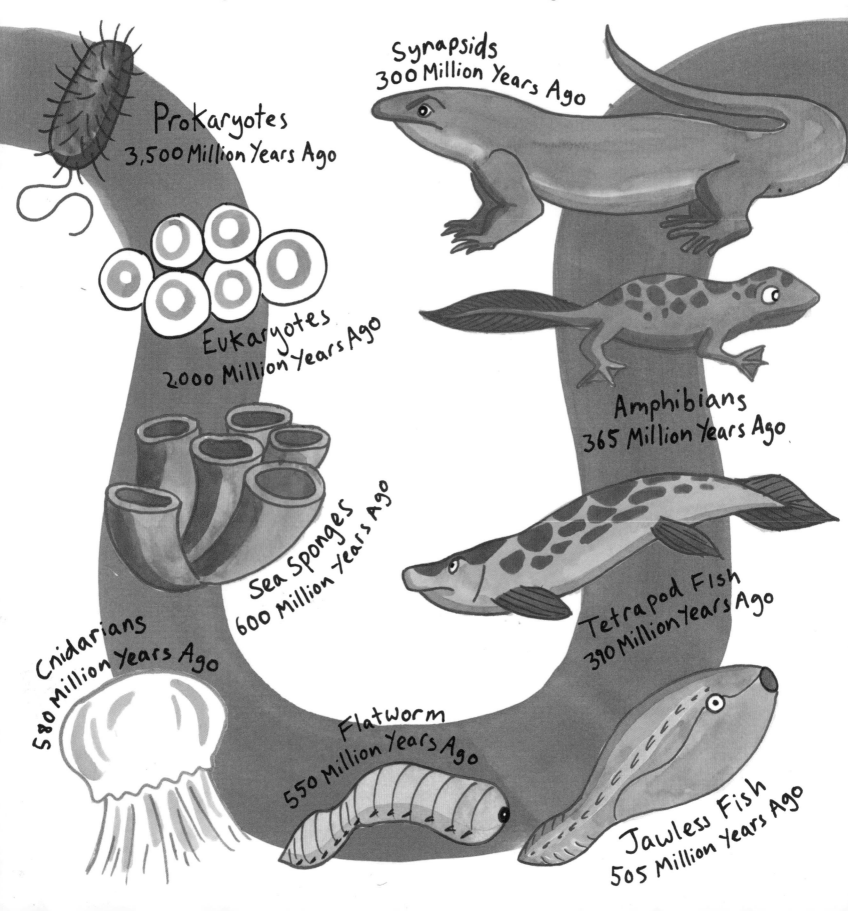

Prokaryotes
3,500 Million Years Ago

Eukaryotes
2,000 Million Years Ago

Sea Sponges
600 Million Years Ago

Cnidarians
580 Million Years Ago

Flatworm
550 Million Years Ago

Jawless Fish
505 Million Years Ago

Tetrapod Fish
390 Million Years Ago

Amphibians
365 Million Years Ago

Synapsids
300 Million Years Ago

EVOLUTION ON EARTH

Evolution is a scientific theory that explains how animals and plants can gradually change over time. Evolution happens very quickly on the Borks' planet and there are big changes each time the Borks have babies.

For Earth animals, the changes are usually much smaller and not so easy to spot. Because Earth animals only change a tiny bit at a time, they take much longer to evolve. It might take an Earth animal millions of years to change as much as the Borks in the story do.

Charles Darwin,
the English scientist who published
his theory of evolution,
On the Origin of Species, in 1859.

Charles Darwin came up with his
theory of evolution after visiting
the Galapagos Islands
in South America.